BRAVE ENOUGH

Also by Cheryl Strayed

Wild: A Journey from Lost to Found

Torch

*Tiny Beautiful Things: Advice on Love and Life
from Someone Who's Been There*

CHERYL STRAYED

BRAVE ENOUGH

A MINI INSTRUCTION MANUAL FOR THE SOUL

ATLANTIC BOOKS
London

First published in hardback in Great Britain in 2015 by Atlantic Books,
an imprint of Atlantic Books Ltd.

10 9 8 7 6 5

A CIP catalogue record for this book is available from the British Library.

Hardback ISBN: 978 1 78239 853 0
E-book ISBN: 978 1 78239 854 7

Printed and bound by CPI Group (UK) Ltd, Croydon, CR0 4YY

Atlantic Books
An Imprint of Atlantic Books Ltd
Ormond House
26–27 Boswell Street
London
WC1N 3JZ

www.atlantic-books.co.uk

For Carver and Bobbi,
who say the best things

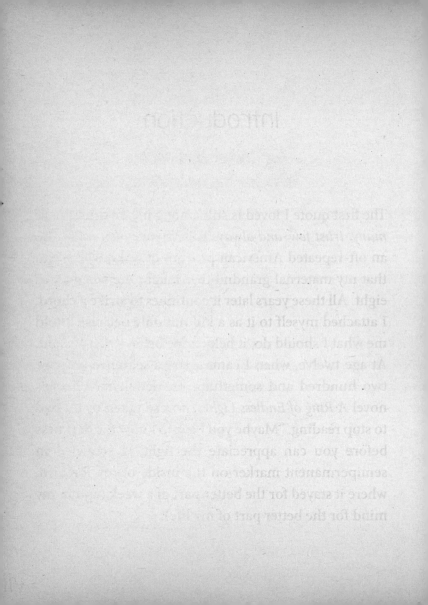

Introduction

The first quote I loved is still among my favorites: *Love many, trust few, and always paddle your own canoe*. It's an oft-repeated American proverb of unknown origin that my maternal grandmother taught me when I was eight. All these years later it continues to strike a chord. I attached myself to it as a kid not only because it told me what I should do; it helped me believe that I could. At age twelve, when I came upon a sentence on page two hundred and something of Madeleine L'Engle's novel *A Ring of Endless Light*, I was so taken by it I had to stop reading. "Maybe you have to know the darkness before you can appreciate the light," I scrawled in semipermanent marker on the inside of my forearm, where it stayed for the better part of a week (and in my mind for the better part of my life).

I've been a quote collector ever since.

From the comic to the profound, the simple to the complex, the sorrowful to the ecstatic, the inspiring to the stern, whenever I need consolation or encouragement, a clear-eyed perspective or a swift kick in the pants – which is often – quotes are what I turn to. They've been tacked to the walls of every home I've made. I've written them down in my journals and kept them in files on my computer. I've scribbled them on the backs of ripped-open envelopes and drawn them across stretches of sand. They appear throughout all three of my previous books. They were a part of my weddings and my blessingways (the hippie/feminist version of baby showers). I read the words of others at my mother's memorial service and had her own words – *I'm always with you* – etched on her gravestone. I've offered quotes as tokens of my affection to lovers and friends in good times and bad. It was a quote of my own making – *I am not afraid* – that carried me through my 1,100-mile hike on the Pacific Crest Trail when I was twenty-six and a quote from my mother – *Put yourself in the way of beauty* – that motivated me to take the journey in the first place. A few years later, as I began in earnest to write my first book, I was driven on by my daily reading of the quotes by Flannery O'Connor and Eudora Welty that I wrote on the chalkboard that sat near my desk. As I labored for more than forty hours while birthing my first child, Ram Dass's advice to *be here now* was a life raft, and it has served me in a different way as I've watched my two children grow at what seems like lightning speed.

I think of quotes as mini-instruction manuals for the soul. It's my appreciation of their very usefulness that compelled me to put together this book. Not because I believe in my own sagacity, but because I believe in the power of words to help us reset our intentions, clarify our thoughts, and create a counternarrative to the voice of doubt many of us have murmuring in our heads – the one that says, *You can't, you won't, you shouldn't have.* Quotes, at their core, almost always shout, *Yes!*

This aims to be a book of yes.

When I made the selections included here – culled from the books and essays I've written and interviews and talks I've given – I remembered that when I first wrote or said them they were not "wisdoms" I wished to bestow upon others. In fact, I never imagined they'd be interpreted as wisdoms at all. Most of the quotes included here feel to me more like conversations I was having with myself that turned out to be conversations other people were apparently having with themselves, too. For every quote in this book imploring you to accept and forgive and be brave (enough), to be kind and grateful and honest, to be generous and bold, I'm imploring myself to do the same.

In other words, I'm not trying to be the boss of you. I'm attempting to be a better boss of me. These quotes are who I am, yes, but they're also who I'm trying to be – a person I fall short of being on a rather regular basis. If you don't believe me, ask my husband. He was once so struck by something I said to him in the course of an argument that he immediately wrote it on a scrap of paper and stuck it to our refrigerator, where it stayed for nearly a decade. The quote? *I'm going to be mad at you for the rest of my life.*

Except I'm pretty sure I said it in ALL CAPS. With an exclamation point!

So you see, I'm very much still a work in progress. Which is exactly what I've known all along – in spite of the tweets, posts, tattoos, quilts, coffee mugs and greeting cards, posters, and needlepoint pillows with my quotes that have cropped up over the past few years. Each time I see words of mine taken up in this way I'm flattered, but surprised.

I'm also reminded of how those words no longer belong only to me; how, when we identify with what another has said or written, we use those words as an articulation of our own inner voices, not only as a celebration of theirs. Winston Churchill was encouraging his countrymen to endure the profound hardships and terrifying uncertainties of World War II when he said, "Never give in", but in the seven-plus decades since he uttered those words, countless people have applied that simple but powerful phrase to inspire them to push through their own struggles, large and small, humble and inane (and, okay, in my case, hiking-related). At my book signings it's become a common request that I inscribe copies of *Tiny Beautiful Things* with variations on my "Write like a motherfucker" quote. *Engineer like a motherfucker,* I've written. *Mother like a motherfucker. Teach like a motherfucker. Doctor like a motherfucker.* And my favorite of all: *Do everything like a motherfucker.*

Which was always, of course, the point.

The best quotes don't speak to one particular truth, but rather to universal truths that resonate – across time, culture, gender, generation, and situation – in our own hearts and minds. They guide, motivate, validate, challenge, and comfort us in our own lives. They reiterate what we've figured out and remind us how much there is yet to learn. Pithily and succinctly, they lift us momentarily out of the confused and conflicted human muddle. Most of all, they tell us we're not alone. Their existence is proof that others have questioned, grappled with, and come to know the same truths we question and grapple with, too.

I hope this book serves that purpose for you. Read it like a motherfucker.

Be brave enough to break your own heart.

We don't reach the
mountaintop
from the mountaintop.

We start at the bottom
and climb up.
Blood is involved.

YOU don't have to get a job that makes others feel comfortable about what they perceive as your success. You don't have to explain what you plan to do with your life. You don't have to justify your education by demonstrating its financial rewards. You don't have to maintain an impeccable credit score. Anyone who expects you to do any of those things has no sense of history or economics or science or the arts. You have to pay your own electric bill. You have to be kind. You have to give it all you've got. You have to find people who love you truly and love them back with the same truth.

But that's all.

Don't surrender all your joy for an idea you used to have about yourself that isn't true anymore.

You're looking for the explanation, the loophole, the bright twist in the dark tale that reverses your story's course. But it won't reverse – for me or for you or for anyone who has ever been wronged, which is everyone. Allow your acceptance of the universality of suffering to be a transformative experience. You do that by simply looking at what pains you squarely in the face and then moving on. **You don't have to move fast or far. You can go just an inch. You can mark your progress breath by breath.**

It isn't too late.

Time is not running out.

Your life is
here
and
now.

And the moment has arrived
at which you're finally
ready to change.

Nobody's going to do your life for you.

You have to do it yourself,
whether you're rich or poor, out of
money or raking it in, the beneficiary
of ridiculous fortune or terrible injustice.
And you have to do it no matter what is true.
No matter what is hard. No matter what unjust,
sad, sucky things have befallen you. Self-pity is
a dead-end road. You make the choice to drive
down it. It's up to you to decide to stay parked
there or to turn around and drive out.

When you recognize that you will thrive not in spite of your losses and sorrows, but because of them, that you would not have chosen the things that happened in your life, but you are grateful for them, that you will hold the empty bowls eternally in your hands, but you also have the capacity to fill them?

The word for that is healing.

Eight of the ten things you have decided about yourself at the age of twenty will, over time, prove to be false. The other two things will prove to be so true that you'll look back in twenty years and howl.

I considered my options.

There was only one, I knew.

There was always only one.

To keep walking.

You can't ride
to the fair
unless you
get on the pony.

You go on by doing the best you can.

You go on by being generous.

You go on by being true.

You go on by offering comfort to
others who can't go on.

You go on by allowing the unbearable days to
pass and by allowing the pleasure in other days.

You go on by finding a channel for your love
and another for your rage.

There are some things you can't understand yet. Your life will be a great and continuous unfolding. It's good you've worked hard to resolve childhood issues while in your twenties, but understand that what you resolve will need to be resolved again. And again.

You will come to know things that can only be known with the wisdom of age and the grace of years.

Most of those things will have to do with forgiveness.

13

It is the plight of almost every monogamous person at one time or another to love **X** but want to fuck **Z**.

We all love **X** but want to fuck **Z**. **Z** is so gleaming, so crystalline, so unlikely to bitch at you for neglecting to take out the recycling. Nobody has to haggle with **Z**. **Z** doesn't wear a watch.

Z is like a motorcycle with no one on it. **Beautiful. Going nowhere.**

Do not reach the era of child-rearing
and real jobs with a guitar case full of crushing
regret for all the things you wished you'd done
in your youth. People who didn't do those things
risk becoming mingy, addled, shrink-wrapped
versions of the people
they intended to be.

Stop asking yourself what you want, what you desire, what interests you. Ask yourself instead: *What has been given to me?* Ask: *What do I have to give back?* Then give it.

Most things will be
okay eventually, but
not everything will be.
Sometimes you'll put up
a good fight and lose.
Sometimes you'll hold on
really hard and realize
there is no choice
but to let go.

**Acceptance is a small,
quiet room.**

You know what I do when I feel jealous? I tell myself not to feel jealous. I shut down the *Why not me?* voice and replace it with one that says *Don't be silly* instead. It really is that easy. You actually do stop being an awful jealous person by stopping being an awful jealous person. When you feel like crap because someone has got something you want you force yourself to remember how very much you have been given. You remember that there is plenty for all of us. You remember that someone else's success has no bearing on your own. You remember that a wonderful thing has happened to someone else and maybe, if you keep working and if you get lucky, something wonderful may also someday happen to you. And if you can't muster that, you just stop. You do not let yourself think about it. **There isn't a thing to eat down there in the rabbit hole of your bitterness except your own desperate heart.**

Transformation doesn't ask that you stop being you. It demands that you find a way back to the authenticity and strength that's already inside of you.

You only have to bloom.

What if I forgave myself?

What if I forgave myself even though I'd done some things I shouldn't have? What if I was sorry, but if I could go back in time I wouldn't do anything different from what I'd done? What if yes was the right answer instead of no? What if all those things I shouldn't have done were what got me here? What if I was never redeemed? What if I already was?

Hello Fear.

Thank you for being here.
You're my indication
that I'm doing what
I need to do.

There are so many tiny revolutions in a life, a million ways we have to circle around ourselves to grow and change and be okay. And perhaps the body is our final frontier. Most women and some men spend their lives trying to alter it, hide it, prettify it, make it what it isn't, or conceal it for what it is. But what if we didn't do that? **What's on the other side of the tiny gigantic revolution in which you move from loathing to loving your own skin?** What fruits would that particular liberation bear?

Believe in the integrity and value of the jagged path. We don't always do the right thing on our way to rightness.

When it comes to our children, we do not have the luxury of despair. If we rise, they will rise with us every time, no matter how many times we've fallen. Remembering that is the most important work we can possibly do as parents.

Romantic love is not a competitive sport.

You're running your own race.
We don't dig or not dig people
based on a comparison chart
of body measurements and
intellectual achievements
and personality quirks.
We dig them because we *do*.

It had only to do with how it felt to be in the wild. With what it was like to walk for miles for no reason other than to witness the accumulation of trees and meadows, mountains and deserts, streams and rocks, rivers and grasses, sunrises and sunsets. The experience was powerful and fundamental. It seemed to me that it had always felt like this to be a human in the wild, and as long as the wild existed it would always feel this way.

Be about ten times more magnanimous than you believe yourself capable of being. Your life will be a hundred times better for it.

An ethical and evolved life entails telling the truth about oneself and living out that truth. Leaving a relationship because you want to doesn't exempt you from your obligation to be a decent human being. You can leave and still be a compassionate friend to your partner. Leaving because you want to doesn't mean you pack your bags the moment there's strife or struggle or uncertainty. It means that if you yearn to be free of a particular relationship and you feel that yearning lodged within you more firmly than any of the other competing and contrary yearnings are lodged, your desire to leave is not only valid, but probably the right thing to do. Even if someone you love is hurt by that.

The people who don't give up are the people who find a way to believe in abundance rather than scarcity. They've taken into their hearts the idea that there is enough for all of us, that success will manifest itself in different ways for different people, that keeping the faith is more important than cashing the check.

If, as a culture, we don't bear witness to grief, the burden of loss is placed entirely on the bereaved, while the rest of us avert our eyes and wait for those in mourning to stop being sad, to let go, to move on, to cheer up. And if they don't – if they have loved too deeply, if they do wake each morning thinking, *I cannot continue to live* – well, then we pathologize their pain; we call their suffering a disease. We do not help them: we tell them that they need to get help.

You will learn a lot from yourself if you stretch in the direction of goodness, of bigness, of kindness, of forgiveness, of emotional bravery.

Be a warrior for love.

You are obliged to tell the people you're sleeping with regularly whether or not you're sleeping with them exclusively. There are no exceptions to this rule. Ever. For anyone. Under any circumstances. People have the right to know if the people they are fucking are also fucking other people. This is the only way the people fucking people who are fucking other people can make emotionally healthy decisions about their lives.

No is golden.

No is the power the
good witch wields.

GRIEF is tremendous, but love is bigger. You are grieving because you loved truly. The beauty in that is greater than the bitterness of death. Allowing this into your consciousness will not keep you from your suffering, but it will help you survive the next day.

Inhabit the beauty that
lives in your beastly body
and strive to see the
beauty in all the
other beasts.

LOVE is the feeling we have for those we care deeply about and hold in high regard. It can be light as the hug we give a friend or heavy as the sacrifices we make for our children. It can be romantic, platonic, familial, fleeting, everlasting, conditional, unconditional, imbued with sorrow, stoked by sex, sullied by abuse, amplified by kindness, twisted by betrayal, deepened by time, darkened by difficulty, leavened by generosity, nourished by humor, and loaded with promises and commitments that we may or may not want or keep. The best thing you can possibly do with your life is to tackle the motherfucking shit out of it.

The useless days will add up to something.

The shitty waitressing jobs. The hours writing in your journal. The long, meandering walks. The days reading poetry and story collections and novels and dead people's diaries and wondering about sex and God and whether you should shave under your arms or not. These things are your becoming.

Walk without a stick into the darkest woods.

The unifying theme is resilience and faith. **The unifying theme is being a warrior and a motherfucker.** It is not fragility. It's strength. It's nerve. And "if your Nerve, deny you —," as Emily Dickinson wrote, "Go above your Nerve."

39

Honor is inconvenient and absolute. Honor is looking it square in the face and taking it on the chin. It's having the guts to break someone's heart so as to avoid fucking with his or her head.

You cannot convince people to love you. This is an absolute rule. No one will ever give you love because you want him or her to give it. Real love moves freely in both directions. Don't waste your time on anything else.

Ask yourself:
What is the best
I can do?
And then do that.

FEAR, to a great extent, is born of a story we tell ourselves, and so I chose to tell myself a different story from the one women are told. I decided I was safe. I was strong. I was brave. That nothing could vanquish me. Insisting on this story was a form of mind control, but for the most part, it worked. Every time I felt something horrible cohering in my imagination, I pushed it away. I simply did not let myself become afraid. Fear begets fear. Power begets power. I willed myself to beget power. And it wasn't long before I actually wasn't afraid.

Withholding love distorts reality. It makes the people who do the withholding ugly and small-hearted. It makes the people from whom things are withheld crazy and desperate and incapable of knowing what they actually feel.

Don't be strategic or coy.

Strategic and coy are for jackasses.

Be brave. Be authentic. Practice saying the word *love* to the people you love, so when it matters the most to say it, you will.

Trust your gut.
Forgive yourself.
Be grateful.

What's important is that you make the leap. Jump high and hard with intention and heart. Pay no mind to the vision that the committee made up. You get to make your life.

You must love in order
to be loved. You must
be inclusive in order to
feel yourself among the
included. You must give in
order to receive.

Desperation is unsustainable.

The question isn't whether you should stay or go. The question is:

How would your life be transformed if you chose to love this time with all your intelligence?

Some facts of your childhood will remain immutable, but others won't. You may never make sense of the bad things that happened to you, but with work and with mindfulness, with understanding and heart, you **will** make sense of yourself.

How wild it was, to let it be.

Fucked-up people will try to tell you otherwise, but boundaries have nothing to do with whether you love someone or not. They are not judgments, punishments, or betrayals. They are a purely peaceable thing: the basic principles you identify for yourself that define the behaviors that you will tolerate from others, as well as the responses you will have to those behaviors.

Boundaries teach people how to treat you and they teach you how to respect yourself.

Every last one of us can do better than give up.

That place of true healing
is a fierce place. It's a giant place.
It's a place of monstrous beauty
and endless dark and glimmering
light. And you have to work really,
really, really hard to get there,
but you can do it.

There is a middle path, but it goes in only one direction: toward the light. Your light. The one that goes *blink, blink, blink* inside your chest when you know what you're doing is right.

You let time pass. That's the cure. You survive the days. You float like a rabid ghost through the weeks. You cry and wallow and lament and scratch your way back up through the months.

And then one day you find yourself alone on a bench in the sun and you close your eyes and lean your head back and **you realize you're okay**.

Forgiveness doesn't
just sit there like a
pretty boy in a bar.

Forgiveness is the
old fat guy you have to
haul up the hill.

The answer to most problems is more often than not outside of the right-wrong binary that we tend to cling to when we're angry or scared or in pain.

We are a complicated people.

Our lives do not play out in absolutes.

In order to set limits successfully one must see the situation for what it is, discern what one wants and is willing to give, and then respectfully communicate those things to the involved parties. Limits are not punishments, but rather lucid and respectful expressions of our needs and desires and capabilities. They allow us to be rational about situations that would otherwise make us froth at the mouth with fury.

When we fail to set healthy limits we become bitter, angry, tiny-hearted people.

LOVE
is our essential nutrient. Without it, life has little meaning. It's the best thing we have to give and the most valuable thing we receive. It's worthy of all the hullabaloo.

**Stop worrying about whether you're fat.
You're not fat. Or, rather, you're sometimes
a little bit fat, but who gives a shit?**
There is nothing more boring and fruitless
than a woman lamenting the fact that her
stomach is round. Feed yourself. Literally.
The sort of people worthy of your love
will love you more for this.

Don't do what you know on a gut level to be the wrong thing to do. **Don't** stay when you know you should go or go when you know you should stay. **Don't** fight when you should hold steady or hold steady when you should fight. **Don't** focus on the short-term fun instead of the long-term fallout. It's hard to know what to do when you have a conflicting set of emotions and desires, but it's not as hard as we pretend it is. Saying it's hard is ultimately a justification to do whatever seems like the easiest thing to do – have the affair, stay at that horrible job, end a friendship over a slight, keep tolerating someone who treats you terribly. **There isn't a single dumbass thing I've done in my adult life that I didn't know was a dumbass thing to do while I was doing it**. Even when I justified it to myself, the truest part of me knew I was doing the wrong thing.

Uncertain as I was as I pushed forward, I felt right in my pushing, as if the effort itself meant something. That perhaps being among the undesecrated beauty of the wilderness meant I, too, could be undesecrated, regardless of what I'd lost or what had been taken from me, regardless of the regrettable things I'd done to others or to myself or the regrettable things that had been done to me. Of all the things I'd been skeptical about, I didn't feel skeptical about this: the wilderness had a clarity that included me.

Don't lament so much about how your career is going to turn out. **You don't have a career. You have a life.** Do the work. Keep the faith. Be true blue. You are a writer because you write. Keep writing and quit your bitching. Your book has a birthday. You don't know what it is yet.

Art isn't anecdote.

It's the consciousness we
bring to bear on our lives.

It was wrong. It was so relentlessly awful that my mother had been taken from me. I couldn't even hate her properly. I didn't get to grow up and pull away from her and bitch about her with my friends and confront her about the things I wished she'd done differently and then get older and understand that she did the best she could and realize that what she did was pretty damn good and take her fully back into my arms again. Her death had obliterated that. It had obliterated me. It had cut me short at the very height of my youthful arrogance. It had forced me to instantly grow up and forgive her every motherly fault at the same time that it kept me forever a child, my life both ended and begun in that premature place where we'd left off. She was my mother, but I was motherless. I was trapped by her but utterly alone. She would always be the empty bowl that no one could fill. I'd have to fill it myself **again** and **again** and **again**.

The thing about rising is we have to continue upward; the thing about going beyond is we have to keep going.

Compassion isn't
about solutions.

It's about giving
all the love that
you've got.

The narratives we create
in order to justify our actions and choices
become in so many ways who we are. They are
the things we say to ourselves to explain our
complicated lives. Perhaps the reason you've
not yet been able to forgive yourself is that
you're still invested in your self-loathing.
**Would you be a better or worse
person if you forgave yourself
for the bad things you did?**
If you perpetually condemn yourself,
does that make you good?

69

We are all entitled
to our opinions and
religious beliefs, but
we are **not** entitled to
make shit up and then use
the shit we made up to
oppress other people.

The greatest truth isn't in the confession, but rather in the lesson learned.

Can I convince the person about whom
I'm crazy to be crazy about me?

The short answer is **no**.
The long answer is **no**.

There are so many things to be tortured about.
So many torturous things in this life. Don't let
someone who doesn't love you be one of them.

I'll never know and neither will you about the life you didn't choose. We'll only know that whatever that sister life was, it was important and beautiful and not ours. It was the ghost ship that didn't carry us.

There's nothing to do but salute it from the shore.

73

Travel by foot.

There is so much
you can't identify at
top speed.

IF someone is being unkind or petty or jealous or distant or weird, you don't have to take it in. You don't have to turn it into a big psychodrama about your worth. That behavior so often is not even about you. It's about the person who's being unkind or petty or jealous or distant or weird. If this were summed up on a bumper sticker, it would say: **Don't own other people's crap**. The world would be a better place if we all did that.

Trust that all you've learned was worth learning, no matter what answer you have or do not have about what practical use it has in your life. Let whatever mysterious starlight that guided you this far guide you onward into the crazy beauty that awaits.

When the path reveals itself, follow it.

The most
terrible
and
beautiful
and
interesting
things happen in a life.
Whatever happens to you belongs
to you. Make it yours. Feed it to
yourself even if it feels impossible
to swallow. Let it nurture you,
because it will.

There are stories hidden in the language we use, whether we're conscious of them or not. They tell the truth of our hearts and minds.

We do not
have the right to
feel helpless. We must help
ourselves. After destiny has
delivered what it delivers,
we are responsible
for our lives.

Accept that their actions hurt you deeply. **Accept** that this experience taught you something you didn't want to know. **Accept** that sorrow and strife are part of even a joyful life. **Accept** that it's going to take a long time for you to get that monster out of your chest. **Accept** that someday what pains you now will surely pain you less.

You can't fake the core.
The truth that lives there
will eventually win out.
It's a god we must obey,
a force that brings us all
inevitably to our knees.
It asks, eternally:
*Will you do it later or
will you do it now?*

We have the capacity
to redraw the lines between
our **powerlessness** and our
power. We're altered by what
hurts us, but with love and
consciousness, with intention
and forgiveness, we can
become whole again.

The whole deal about loving truly and for real and with all you've got has everything to do with letting those we love see us. Silence makes hard things harder than they need to be. It creates a secret you're too beautiful to keep. Telling has a way of dispersing things.

This isn't a spotless life. There is much ahead, my immaculate peach.

Let fall your notions about "perfect couples." It's such an impossible thing to either perceive honestly in others or live up to when others believe it about us. It does nothing but box some people in and shut other people out, and it ultimately makes just about everyone feel like shit. A perfect couple is a wholly private thing. No one but the two people in the perfect relationship know for certain whether they're in one. Its only defining quality is that it's composed of two people who feel perfectly right about sharing their lives with each other, even during the hard times.

Parents teach their children how to be warriors, to give them the confidence to get on the horse to ride into battle when it's necessary to do so. If you didn't get that from your parents, you have to teach yourself.

The story of human intimacy is one of constantly allowing ourselves to see those we love most deeply in a new, more fractured light.

Look hard.

Risk that.

My advice to my adolescent self?

You know who you are, so let yourself be her now. It's okay to be smart and ambitious and curious and not terribly cool. Don't waste all those years trying to get the boys to want you and the girls to like you. Don't starve yourself skinny. Don't be a pretty cheerleader. Don't lose your virginity to the captain of the football team. Don't lose anything to him. Be the captain. You are the captain.

Take the ball and run.

Go because
you want to go.
Because wanting to
leave is enough.

You have to say
"I am forgiven"
again and again
until it becomes the
story you believe
about yourself.

The other side of
fearlessness is fear.

The other side of
strength is fragility.

The other side of
power is faith.

It's in the most basic, essential, beginning stories that so much of our lives are written. Who loved you best? What made you finally believe in yourself? From what garden or pot or crack in the pavement did you grow? How did you get your water?

We are all at risk of something. Of ending up exactly where we began, of failing to imagine and find and know and actualize who we could be. **We all need to jump from here to there. The only difference among us is the distance of the leap.**

The particularity of our problems can be made bearable only through the recognition of our universal humanity.

We suffer uniquely, but we survive the same way.

If love were an animal,
it would be two:
a **hummingbird**
and a **snake**.
Both are
perfectly untrainable.

Alone

had always felt like an
actual place to me, as if it
weren't a state of being,
but rather a room where
I could retreat to be
who I really was.

God is not a
granter of wishes.

God is a
ruthless bitch.

If it is impossible for you to go on as you were before, so you must go on as you never have.

Our work, our job, the most important
gig of all, is to make a place that belongs to us,
a structure composed of our own moral code.
Not the code that echoes imposed cultural
values, but the one that tells us on a
visceral level what to do.

How worthless, how weak, how vanquished, how hollow it is to have a parent who exists but cannot reach, who says but will not be, who thinks but doesn't dare, who plays and plays and plays, but only, always, forever in the minor key. We sing the song of parenthood only in the major notes.

Were you there?
Did you love full-throttle?
Did you fix it after you fucked it up?

Cultivate an understanding that life is long, that people both change and remain the same, that **every last one of us will need to fuck up and be forgiven**, that we're all just walking and walking and walking and trying to find our way, that all roads lead eventually to the mountaintop.

Put yourself in the way of beauty.

Bravery is
acknowledging your fear
and doing it anyway.

Most people don't cheat because they're cheaters. They cheat because they're people. They are driven by hunger or for the experience of someone being hungry once more for them. They find themselves in friendships that take an unintended turn or they seek them out because they're horny or drunk or damaged from all the stuff they didn't get when they were kids. There is love. There is lust. There is opportunity. There is alcohol. And youth. And middle age. There is loneliness and boredom and sorrow and weakness and self-destruction and idiocy and arrogance and romance and ego and nostalgia and power and need. There is the compelling temptation of intimacies with someone other than the person with whom one is most intimate. Which is a complicated way of saying it's a long damn life. And people get mucked up in it from time to time.

Even the people we marry.

Even us.

We all like to think
we're right about what we believe
about ourselves and what we often
believe are only the best, most
moral things. We like to pretend
that our generous impulses
come naturally.

**But the reality is we often
become our kindest, most
ethical selves only by seeing
what it feels like to be selfish
assholes first.**

Healing is a small and
ordinary and very burnt
thing. And it's one thing
and one thing only:
it's doing what you
have to do.

To love and be loved.

That is the meaning of life.

The body knows.
When your heart sinks.
When you feel sick to
your gut. When something
blossoms in your
chest. When your brain
gloriously pops. That's
your body telling you
the One True Thing.

Listen to it.

NOBODY will protect you from your suffering. You can't cry it away or eat it away or starve it away or walk it away or punch it away or even therapy it away. It's just there, and you have to survive it. You have to endure it. You have to live through it and love it and move on and be better for it and run as far as you can in the direction of your best and happiest dreams across the bridge that was built by your own desire to heal. Therapists and friends can help you along the way, but the healing — the genuine healing, the actual real-deal, down-on-your-knees-in-the-mud change — is entirely and absolutely up to you.

Our most meaningful relationships are often those that continued beyond the juncture at which they came closest to ending.

Real change
happens on the
level of the gesture.
It's one person
doing one thing
differently than
he or she has
done it before.

Work hard.

Do good.

Be incredible.

This is not
how your story ends.
It's simply where
**it takes a turn
you didn't expect.**

You don't have to be young. You don't have to be thin. You don't have to be "hot" in a way that some dumbfuckedly narrow mind-set has construed that word. You don't have to have taut flesh or a tight ass or an eternally upright set of tits. You have to find a way to inhabit your body while enacting your deepest desires. You have to be brave enough to build the intimacy you deserve. You have to take off all of your clothes and say, *I'm right here*.

This is not the moment
to wilt into the
underbrush of your
insecurities.

You've earned the
right to grow.

Ultimatums have negative connotations for many because they're often used by bullies and abusers, who tend to be comfortable pushing people's backs against a wall, demanding that others choose this or that, all or nothing. But when used right, ultimatums offer a respectful and loving way through an impasse that would sooner or later have destroyed a relationship on its own anyway. They require us to ask for something we need from someone else, yes, but they demand the most from us. They require us to acknowledge that the worst-case scenario – the end of a cherished relationship – is better than the alternative – a lifetime of living with sorrow and humiliation and rage. They demand that we ask of ourselves: *What do I want? What do I deserve? What will I sacrifice to get it?* And then they require that we do it. In fear and in pain and in faith, to swim there.

We all get stuck in place on occasion.
We all move backward sometimes.
Every day we must make the decision to
move in the direction of our intentions.

Forward is the direction of real life.

Your assumptions about the lives of others
are in direct relation to your naïve pomposity.

Many people you believe to be rich are not rich.

Many people you think have it easy
worked hard for what they got.

Many people who seem to be gliding right
along have suffered and are suffering.

The universe,
I'd learned, was never,
ever kidding.

It would take whatever it
wanted and it would never
give it back.

You don't have a right
to the cards you
believe you should
have been dealt.

You have an obligation
to play the hell
out of the ones
you're holding.

YOU are a mortal being like every human and june bug, like every black bear and salmon. We're all going to die, but only some of us are going to die tomorrow or next year or in the next half-century. And, by and large, we don't know which of us it will be when and of what. That mystery is not the curse of our existence; it's the wonder. It's what people are talking about when they talk about the circle of life that we're all part of whether we sign up to be or not – the living, the dead, those being born right at this moment, and the others who are fading out. Attempting to position yourself outside the circle isn't going to save you from anything. It isn't going to keep you from your grief or protect those you love from theirs when you're gone. It isn't going to extend your life or shorten it. **You're here. So be here. You're okay with us for now.**

Something is always at stake. Our integrity. Our serenity. Our relationships. Our communities. Our children. Our ability to bear the weight of the people we hope to be and to forgive the people we are. Our obligation to justice, mercy, kindness, and *doing the stuff in bed that genuinely gets us off.*

Vulnerability is strength.

Acceptance has everything to do with simplicity, with sitting in the ordinary place, with bearing witness to the plain facts of our lives, with not just starting at the essential, but ending up there.

Acceptance speaks in the gentlest voice. It commands only that we acknowledge what's true.

It's folly to measure your success in money or fame. Success is measured only by your ability to say yes to these two questions:

Did I do the work I needed to do?

Did I give it everything I had?

We were all sluts
in the '90s

ONE ends a romantic relationship while remaining a compassionate friend by being kind above all else. By explaining one's decision to leave the relationship with love and respect and emotional transparency. By being honest without being brutal. By expressing gratitude for what was given. By taking responsibility for mistakes and attempting to make amends. By acknowledging that one's decision has caused another human being to suffer. By suffering because of that. By having the guts to stand by one's partner even while one is leaving. By talking it all the way through and by listening. By honoring what once was. By bearing witness to the undoing and salvaging what one can. By being a friend, even if an actual friendship is impossible. By having good manners. By considering how one might feel if the tables were turned. By going out of one's way to minimize hurt and humiliation. By trusting that the most compassionate thing of all is to release those we don't love hard enough or true enough or big enough or right. By believing **we are all worthy of hard, true, big, right love**. By remembering while letting go.

Humility is about
refusing to get all
tangled up with yourself.
It's about surrender,
receptivity, awareness,
simplicity.

Breathing in.

Breathing out.

Trusting yourself means living out what you already know to be true.

I used to see a butterfly in my mind's eye every time I heard the word *transformation*, but life has schooled me. **Transformation isn't a butterfly**. It's the thing before you get to be a pretty bug flying away. It's huddling in the dark cocoon and then pushing your way out. It's the messy work of making sense of your fortunes and misfortunes, desires and doubts, hang-ups and sorrows, actions and accidents, mistakes and successes, so you can go on and become the person you must next become.

Ask better questions,
sweet pea.

The fuck is your life.

Answer it.